MW01520443

Nestle In: poems for hope and inspiration
Written by Stef Guilly @2020
Cover photo by Stef Guilly @2020
Internal photos by Stef Guilly
Back cover photo by Liz Pittman @2019
Edmonton, Alberta Canada
Poems written in 2017, 2018, and 2020

ISBN: 9798554565724
Independently published

Nestle In

By Stef Guilly

Author's Note:

You will see no titles on the poems' pages, and this is a purposeful decision to help you engage with awareness and feelings towards the pieces.

As with all my work, I invite you to interact with the poetry, building on it and using it as a source of inspiration and code for your life. This includes the exploration of the title or main ideas.

If you love the title on the page, I invite you to take beautiful pens and draw the title in your own way. If you love holding a book in your hand, I invite you to mindfully take the extra time to flip the table of contents.

I invite you to interact with the pieces in your own way. I invite you to feel and I invite you to play.

From my heart to yours,

Stef Guilly

This book is for the dreamers:

May you never believe them

when they say that it cannot be done

May you keep your dreams forever

and create new ideas

until your ideas blossom

into Spring across the whole world

May you never forget that

what you are seeking is seeking you

May you remember who you are.

Contents

My words
falling into the hearts
of those who need them
nestle in.

As I settle into my seat,
my place in the world
just for today

I pause
purposefully
and extend my smile

to the morning

hello mother sun, have you come to light my path
once again?

goodbye father moon, thank you for the gift of rest
and reprieve

it is a new day, a blessed day full of possibilities,
synchronicities, and friendship

I am in awe and in gratitude.

What destroys me is
hearing about my friend's depression
not because it's a burden
oh no
not because it weighs on me too
but
I see my friend as a hero
as having it all together
having all the success and the
things
having achieved the daily self control
to do the habits
to get to her goals
and her depression makes me feel
uneasy
If I could hold a mirror up
maybe she could see
how wonderful she is
but I have no mirror
what do I have?
my words. My vision for a clear day.
Can I use my words to heal her heart?
I try
my great desire
is for the world to live free of depression
and for us to remember the world of light.

It's been ages since I've thought about
them, these words
After a big project I dive deep and deeper
into the dark depths of what's next
and what if
I can never do better than that?

Stop go. Stop go. Hurry up and wait.
This space feels like everything I fear
closed, judgmental, and alone

I think back
only a few months ago I was open and thriving
and connected. Now, here I am alone.
As happiness evades, my routine crumbles
slowly and I stand

          in the wake of my destruction
knowing it is time to clean house
to move again into a routine
and to make time for me.
If I can feel deeply proud of achieving,
I can feel the deep shame of not.

Standing taking stock
seems so trivial
but we need to recover our energies
just as much as we need to use them

so, standing taking stock
I look out from the top of the mountain
and I see the expansiveness
of the valleys, valleys I never thought I'd ever cross
on the way to my destination.

I see all the bogs
   That had captured me for months
               years, in some cases

I see the blue sky and the moon shining bright
my constant beacon no matter where I stand

I see the paths that brought me closer by bringing me
further away from my goal and I remember myself
frustrated and bruised, alone, and feeling with no
direction

I see those moments and how they fuelled me
forward, pushing me to seek community and
connection and in the end those people, so bright,
lit a path to my destination

I see the moments I missed and how those saved me
from making bigger mistakes
And here I am in all my glory

At the top of the mountain

finally

My bird brain chatters, "what's next, what's next?"

My gracious heart forces my body to take a minute
and really sink into this moment

I breathe and my lungs, constant companions
soothe me

I gaze across the mountains' edge and look, really
look, I mean, really look at all that I've done to make
it to where I stand today

Oh

    Ooooooh

        Yes!!!! I am a queen!

      It's ok to be proud of myself

       in fact, it's just what I need

         there is beauty is everything.

I know

I remember

I am ok

I know

I remember

I am love

I know

I remember

I am divine

When winter comes, I feel it in my bones

I can tolerate exactly 14 days of collecting my scarves
and boots and sweaters until I crack, and the novelty
of winter drops off

This new introspection of my own reactions to the
seasons
have come about as in my maturity, I can see
past the present moment.

I wonder if using poetry
as a system of moving through seasons
will prove an exercise in futility

since most of what I do
is intuitive

Oh, there, there. Nothing is ever wasted.

Why are we so afraid of change when change is all
we've ever known?

Winter, probably.

Is it love
if she doesn't read
my poems?
Is it love
if we don't paint
together?
Is it love
when the chores
go unnoticed?
Is it love?

When I was young
I used to try on boyfriends
like I was trying on pants
I liked boys who could dance
who weren't in a friend's group,
not a sports fan
let me change the music in the car

my grandfather asked me,
"Would you go out with anyone who asked?"
his tone implied that the correct answer was no.
YES! Of course, I said.
an opportunity to meet someone new
to see a different side of life
plus eating dinner? How delightful

I never wanted a boyfriend
I didn't know what that meant
to be
to be me
to be me with someone else
I wasn't a very good partner
and most of those boys didn't want
to get to know me or explore more
than their sexuality
I actually wasn't ready
but I went along with it
because I didn't know what ready meant

We go through so much of life
without an explanation
I didn't want a boyfriend
        what I wanted to was to be
                my own friend
in a really nice restaurant

I wasted time then and I'm wasting it now
being really pissed off that
the world never told me that
I could have my own time

Now, I'm raging over time
that I'll never have back
there is more than one way to heal from loneliness
and there is more to love than someone else
a relationship isn't not
the answer to everything you lack
I thought that someone should tell you so

You deserve to know.

The sadness
is a river deep inside a mountain
inside the ocean
where my soul resides
a poet sits on the river shore
as the river whispers its fears
and its joys
what is the river?
the sum of many moving parts
promises and disappointments
the river feels its rocks
like knives digging in

What if
we did actually live
in the Matrix
I think we do
maybe without spaceships
(though recently that was
explored by Netflix)

what if
our collective consciousness
is shifting
no more power ballads
just us and songs that come pre-mixed

what if
the split between the people
grows so that one doesn't know the other
exists
I grow weary thinking I am the only one
who sees the shift
everyone is still buying lotto tickets

what if
we transformed the Earth in our lifetime?
healed the broken hearts through love and forgiveness

What if…

I was so scared and
my biggest regret is that
I lost time because of it

In my darkest day I thought
that I had to be alone
I have made it up by the display
of enthusiasm and joyfulness
but my anger fuels me still
anger onto a culture that told me
I had to do it alone, missing the
births and deaths of my sisters
and their children
that I had to labour alone and suffer alone
and travel alone so that I would be
exhausted and easy to own

when I burn low, I come up with ideas and loneliness
the loneliness helps me too
it is all self-imposed

how can a poet write without
heartbreak as her muse?
oh, those years of stitching
words and phrases as tight as barbed wire
across my heart and locking her up alone

I have to let it go
so that I do not suffer twice

Life is short
one minute you are lying the couch
recovering
and the next minute it has been years
of lying on the couch
recovering
hiding from thunderstorms

we forget the purpose of our lives
our soul's mission
we get do caught up in the way
the world wants us to buy
all the treasures and keep them
in our houses, sparkly and clean

did I have time to curate
or cultivate an addiction?
a thunderstorm rages outside
and inside my body

sometimes, I start to make a speech and people listen
to me and I just think - who am I to speak?
I don't know anything

what do I sound like to others? I have forgotten who I
am so many times

affirmations are exhausting
they take so much of your energy

so do creaky beds and worn pillows and tired feet and
messages to return and appointments to book and the
world to live in

get to a place on the ground where you can grow
roots, they said, a family home
your own family home, they said, get your affairs in
order they said and don't forget to purchase all we
have for your happiness

and don't forget to smile

I am in a thunderstorm

I want to watch it but I'm scared, questioning myself:
do I have a mental illness or am I just extremely
sensitive to thunderstorms?

I am in a thunderstorm
I have learned how to survive by doing only the exact
opposite of what culture has taught me to do: think of
the future like a friend and treat it kindly

I am a thunderstorm
I rage together with all the parts of me in perfect
harmony

I am not afraid anymore – not afraid of taking up
space

of using space

and of stopping anytime I want.

I am a thunderstorm.

Watch out for me.

I do not want to exist
in this messy world
of things
layers and wisps
of lies and emotion
used and useless
strewn along
flicked into tree branches
stomped on sidewalks
I come I pick them up
They tangle in my hair
tears collect
our world is created
with words, promises,
emotions, and impulses
when we are strong
our creation reflects
happiness
when we are weak
we favour disconnection
I want to go where
no one has ever been
to be free from
scattered energy
and I know that this place
exists because I've seen it
in my dreams
I have met the version of me
who only sings

All my life is such
a shame
mistake fall mistake oversight
joy
mistake fall mistake oversight
drunk and forget to call.

but maybe joy

joy

JOY!

and then traffic

When I am famous
I will communicate in the most
mysterious and confusing ways

first, I will send only letters
to fans, friends, and family
writing my heart out as my voice
for at least five years

second, I will dive into the world
of smells and cultivate them everywhere
roses, lavender, French cream, gianduja, and Sicilian
blood orange for several years

and in the end, I will practice
the ancient art of secret keeping
and I will free my fans and family and friends
by practicing the sacred act of listening.

Is the coffee finished already?
It feels like I have only taken three sips
I check the time
   An hour has danced away, one minute at a time
I feel into my body
actually
I have had enough coffee
   A deep unease has drifted into my belly
no food, only coffee is an acidic way to greet my
body in the morning
     how many times?
I close my eyes and my eyelids seal
With a thud
Like a broken garage door

The opening button is coffee
The car is coffee
The house is coffee
The floor is lava

Why are there so many steps involved in being alive?
Who is the beneficiary of all my labour, anyway?

I'd like to take a day off today… who do I call? what
papers do I sign? how can I get away?

What I can say?
my role is of a truth-teller
and why shouldn't I?
relationships are tricky
two people, sovereign countries
together to potentially raise
more sovereign creatures
in a state of hyper-arousal
a police-state of stress
(and this year includes a pandemic)
and some of us have stronger maps
to bring ourselves back to each other
and some of us have broken maps
that have never proved effective
we use them regardless because our
parents gave us them
and you wouldn't return a gift,
    how rude!
we barrel on
barely hanging on some days
and I don't know what to do
and I feel like I've been had
by movies promising me
a constant sky
of blue
sometimes, I don't know what to do

Will I remember any of this
        in my next life?

Have I remembered everything?
Will I ever?

Am I anything?

Or am I everything.

Stardust.

       Consciousness.

                Pure love.

He would say that I am everything
the way the sand makes the dessert
but one piece of sand, of crystal, of stardust
is probably your neighbor
       he one who is an asshole
and you are made of the same star stuff as he

and I wonder if my neighbour is helping themselves
out from a previous lifetime too.

I brought my hedgehog across the city on the train to
my mother's house.

I know you have to be more aware of her
like how the sun shines on her
and I joked to my mom as we discussed the garden of
kale

- is being a mom like this - where a part of you is
always wondering about her ambient temperature?
and it is. because 5 seconds later my mom starts
asking me if I want a hat. and I mean starts because in
3 minutes she will go get the hat. she just asks ... then
keeps on describing all the hats she owns until you
choose one.
so, you had better just choose.

so, I get a hat and then I laugh because that's exactly
what it's like.

and talking about its poop. where, when and why and
being excited about it.
mom she pooped in your garden!
and I am relieved about that.

Charlotte's Garden 2018

When you are ready
you try to find yourself again
you leave yourself a code - some hang up or
annoyance or yearning for something you don't
understand. It comes into your life
enveloped in mystery
it is never the thing that you think.
Would you know if you saw her?
the one you become when it is all done
would you have left yourself
a note from future you?
Who is more of a stranger
at this point in your evolution?
shrug. how many of us are
strangers to ourselves
in present day?
it really should not be a surprise
this universal gift of synchronicity
as strange as it seems
one day you will want to seek yourself out
and you will find that your path has always been lit
up by fairy lights and roses
simply waiting for you to step forward
and claim what has always been yours.

We celebrate and adore
those who learn to sing
and bring their authentic
voices to the world
the idea starts in childhood
that to be good one must
be good at something
music, math, or art
and if you are without a
natural talent, you go seeking
always wishing you could
bring something out at
parties like that girl who
knows all the Jack Johnson songs
we celebrate those who can
cultivate different aspects of themselves
on the stage or show up
in different ways
we love so much
not ourselves but
the idea of showing up as someone else
we adorn some of us like goddesses
and celebrate at the academy
we forget and so please don't forget
we are all works of art and
you do not need a thing
to be worth a life of creativity and dignity

A funeral is a sad episode
of "where are they now"
but reversed
and without support
there is simply
no fun about it at all

a celebration of life
is not really a celebration
because the guest of honor
no longer appears

can we just make a space
where we do not have to pretend
that things are fun nor pretend
that we do not simply want to be sad?

can we just make a space
where tears can fall for a million years?
and sadness can comfort our hearts
for the ones who are no longer
why do we feel that we have to be alone in our grief?

Please, let's stop this together
and let's get real we need to talk about it, to listen,
and to feel:
we need connection in order to heal.

When I am alone

I think

Mantra. Mantra. Pause.

other times I think and let it go

let it go,
        let it go

I am exhausted.

when I am alone

I think

am I vain to ponder my own thoughts?

let it go,

        let it go,
           let it go.

He says, you used to dress nicer.
and I look down.

my tights and flip flops,
my oversize dress
the wind sticks it to my body
a swollen stomach,
wider thighs.
I do remember the times
in our mating season
my growing collection of shoes
displayed in my closet
time taken to prepare myself
anticipate
greet butterflies in my stomach
how playful love makes the stomach.
can't eat, can't sleep.
and now,
swollen belly from evenings out
shoes chosen for comfort
the shape of my thighs
the unshape

of love.

You have been
in my thoughts and my heart
it's like bits of you are floating through the air
and there is a smell or a noise
somehow the rush of water
and I see your smile
and I remember us at your kitchen
and now the world seems lighter and at ease
your energy is pure and beautiful
maybe that's what the old poets meant
when they compared people to trees and mountains
and things.

In each moment, you stand
in a trilogy of love and worth
in all your glory, together as a unit

Do not say to your mind: go away
and block your thoughts

Do not say to your body: stop wanting
and starve your body

Do not say to your dreams: stop being
foolish and not listen

That is not love; that is control

love says: mind come gently
let's sit together
body, what do you need?
heart, here, let me listen to you
let's play
love is the mother we all want and deserve

there is time for all of it:
mind, body, and heart
may they all sit at your table in unity

How do you cultivate your heart?
play
create
laugh with friends
how do you cultivate your body?
love it
tell yourself nice things
meditate on its positive qualities
thank it for keeping you alive
stretch it
strengthen it
find a home in it
how do you cultivate your mind?
feed it knowledge, not information
sit with it in silence
accept that it is part of you
how do you cultivate a soul?
poetry is the soul's language
plant seeds of inspiration and water them
with love and time
you will wake up to find blossoms in your mouth
born from the times you "did nothing"
from nothingness comes our greatest work

We stopped into a store named
stationary laundromat
in the basement
                  off the beaten path
half expecting a real laundromat,
   we were greeted by paper

the shopkeeper
she called all the pages of her journals
from their respective corners of the shop
she invited me to touch
hard and serious
soft and comforting
lines that shape the story
and no lines for the stories
that shape themselves
the shopkeeper and I bonded
over experiences that cannot be
shipped and delivered
my heart said our fingers crave to touch,
our soul craves to taste
in a stationary laundromat
  on a quiet Wednesday afternoon,
        my heart sang in gratitude for paper.

I never noticed that

my feet didn't touch the ground

dangling

     never grounded

        not able

                  to rest
on the bus, I could make them touch, only by my
tippy toes

in restaurants, my feet absentmindedly searched for
the table legs
waiting, always waiting for the chair that would allow
my feet to rest

waiting, always waiting

     not sure what I have been waiting for
A little chair, a little stool, a little reprieve
     a little piece of ground
for a place they could call home

stable and solid to place my dreams

sleep? my healer told me that I am not rooted in
sleep
I am not rooted and how could I be?
my feet
never knew the comfort of grounding down
and connecting to earth's bountiful love

dear feet, I notice you now
    I understand that you haven't felt quite right
in this world
as if this world has been built for someone else
anyone else but you

it's not true.

we are here together, you and I

I will take care of you.

I've never met a peppermint tea I didn't like

Men are taught that marriage
is a house to play in and that it is stable
a little lawn moving here and an updated
bathroom there and you have all the things
you'll ever need
that is a lie

women are taught that marriage
is safety net something fragile and
full of opportunity to practice patience and empathy
and listening and personal growth
that is a lie

marriage, he said, is something that women
complicate. They always want men to change.
men just want to be loved for who they are.
marriage, they said, nothing will change when we get
married. We have a great relationship now; I don't
see why that won't continue. The same, the same.

with blinders on to the work involved, we slowly
march down the aisle
the women say more towards the change
we do speak about the power and control
and keeping our access to resources
never depend, my sisters whisper
at the same time, braiding my hair like Rapunzel's,
singing songs from stories about princes who whisk a

beautiful princess to happily ever after where she is
always treated with respect and dignity
that is a lie

why are we lying to each other about what marriage
is about? Why are we keeping secrets and not telling
the truth?
marriage is a boat in the ocean
of life with one eye on the future and one eye in the
present and love to anchor when the seas get to scary
but it's ok because you have a common idea about
where to go and you are grateful and happy to get
there together
marriage is the water that grows you
as you age and transition and get to know
both yourself and someone else more intimately

marriage is also the uniting of resources
of families, of community, of connection
and support when it is thriving or a lack
and isolation and loneliness when it is surviving
marriage is truth telling and nurturing and playful and
fun and creative, that is true
and it can be soul-crushing and empty and blue
and even more if all the souls around you tell you
that marriage is expected of you
marriage is not a woman who complies
that is not what we agree to

Marriage is two souls on a journey together

Not one soul who takes on the responsibilities of the
housework, chores, social obligations, celebrations,
funerals, meals and planning, kid raising and all that
without a previous contract
marriage is not a man getting a woman for his life.
That is not the obligation of a wife.
that is not what we agree to.

we have needs out of marriages that we get to see to,
this is our contract too, this is our life
who controls the idea and identity of a wife?
a wife can decide where she survives and she can
decide to move to where she thrives
at any time and without excuses
and believed with or without showing bruises
or having to open her life up, letting parlour curtains
hang wide so everyone gets to have a look inside,
forced to turn the light on even in the middle of the
darkest night
to those who would say they were family or friends.

marriage was but this not what marriage is today.

marriage is a new way of peaceful exploration and a
quest for adventure, carrying a backpack of respect
and servitude, bathed in love while hiking up a
mountain together

marriage is something new

Men, listen, you cannot take a relationship and try to
fix it to stay in the relationship shell forever
a crab, a lobster, a snail all need new shells in order to
grow

a marriage is not a house built for two that once is
built will no longer fall
a marriage is a jump together.
and the celebration of milestones and
accomplishments, a cheerleader, a friend
and then, a lover
Men expect that first, of course, I'm sorry to say that
the advertisement lied

Women, listen, you do not have to accept a role of
servitude to serve a mission of a hostess for someone
else's life

You can decide.

marriage is a cozy sanctuary,
a place to come home to
if you are a woman who marries another woman,
marriage of course is for you too

marriage is the anchor of the ship in the storm,
while the water rocks us awake,
helping us to rest to see a new day

Swiftly calibrating
slush or ice or
a bank of soft snow
one misstep and
my toes are soaking wet

do I consider nature my enemy?
I look up
the frost gently caresses the trees
their branches sparkle in a lover's embrace
love makes the world sparkle
no, nature is not my enemy

I judge my misstep as

careless

a mistake

doomed
my fault for not paying attention

these labels are the enemy
    drawing me away from
the
crisp fresh sir
imparting my cheers with its gift of crimson
a reminder that I am alive

a l i v e

just like the falling snow,
glistening
playing hide and go seek
winking mischievously
as it disappears
  just as soon as the camera clicks

it reminds us that
the moment
cannot be thought about
analyzed, judged, captured
qualified, quantified

our thoughts and behaviours
distract us from mindful peaceful living
accepting things as they are
not as friends or foes

but as the
          essential essence of being

Mindfulness is

emphasizing

spaces between the
judgements
   the "shoulds"
               "musts"
of our labelling mind's
obsession
with what is
normal, regular, safe

in the space there
lies freedom
      dance
            movement
choice

for some, freedom is
paralyzing, exposed, agoraphobic

a life without boundaries
too many choices
and too many opportunities
to be different
            outcast

notice what it is

what is discomfort?

               how does it feel in the body?

sharp   hot
     vibrant
     blistering   stifling
a monkey on your back
     water that is too warm
we wear a blanket of anxiety

we fear *feeling*   feelings!

as if we can catch them like an illness
or tattoo - permanently etched into our being

notice how fear is temporary
where there is fear there is a choice to view other
options

hope
freedom
mindfulness is choice

 look for the spaces in discomfort and

choice

to feel through life differently

Do you ever ask your partner, "How are you? Are
you enjoying your experience? Are you satisfied in
life?"
these questions are scary because what if, what if
                        the answer is something we don't
want to hear
even more terrifying is asking ourselves
(so we don't)
                we hide our discomfort by little
complaints
these potatoes need more gravy, this wasn't a perfect
meal
and that woman was wearing the wrong dress for the
occasion

do you ever answer, "I am satisfied!"
Or more courageously, "I am grateful"
Where there is fear, there is an opportunity to heal.

do you ever ask yourself, "How are you? Are you
enjoying your experience?"

If the answer is no, you don't have to do it alone, no,
there are places to help you and you deserve it, you
know.

We argue because
time is precious
how little we have
and in love, time goes so fast
we get caught up in
your way or my way
debating why and because
efficiencies to save time
    to what end?
less time doing things?
       stop lover
I don't need less time doing things
what I need is
more time
skin to skin
observing the lines that mark
where you have been
memorizing the turned down crevice
nestled beside your lip
where your apprehension lives
in its cavern of constant vigilance
stop these circles
that we are drawing in the air
and let's hide out together
under covers and be bare.

What kind of tree would you be?
I wouldn't be a coniferous tree
with its edgy spikes
held close to its heart
that wouldn't be me
I would be a tree
that breathes deeply with my leaves
dangling in the wind
he thinks about who I would be
he says you would be
a tree with roots for arms
swinging down, planting
and replanting yourself deeper each year
toes long and thin
each piece placed precariously
under the soil
I finish, 'and ready for adventure!" with a grin
if I were a tree, I would know the seasons
as intimately as a lover and greet them
as a friend
   rain to dance with
      sun to bask in
         snow to soak my weary feet
the great winds of fall to help me bear it all
and a hundred years of sleep

FOR ANGER
DO SOMETHING EXPLOSIVE
IT NEEDS TO GET OUT
ANYTHING, LIKE POPPING BUBBLES
IMMEDIATELY
AS SOON AS YOU ARE AWARE
DO SOMETHING
FOR SELF-CARE
A BALANCE NEEDS TO COME
THREE ACTS INTO ONE
HEALING REQUIRES A DIFFERENT KIND OF
RATIO
BECAUSE YOU ARE HEALING FROM THE
TRAUMA, THE ANGER
AND ALSO, FROM THE SCAR

I used to think that every thought
was a beautiful flower to be cultivated
and worried about
mostly worried about and listed out as the work left to
do and the pressure I put on myself to measure my
worth on the work that is left to do
instead of the work that has been completed
it nearly destroyed me
I recognize that it is a calculation error to measure
worth based on the amount of work left to do and I
challenge you to correct that error too.

We are worthy even if we did nothing ever
how does that sit with you?
thoughts are weeds in our gardens
or simply stray growth
we are the writers of our story,
the editors of our life
we choose what grows in our garden
snip snip snip
trim up your hair
cut your nails
snip snip snip
think happy thoughts

[note: gratitude is not a distress tolerance skill and
happy thoughts are not a replacement for professional
support]

Do you think someone's outside appearance
is a direct reflection of their internal world?
yes?
so, it would be quite distressing to you
to see someone like me
with all my fat and all my rolls on display
for all to see
you think that my laundry is soiled
and I am displaying it to the world
not only that but much more
much more judgement like selfish
as in it's selfish to eat more than your share
and don't you know when to stop?
don't you know how to stop
picking apart a life?

to be able to have self-control is to have
developed a sense of self - what is ok and what is not
hardly a small feat
I am a miracle and my body is me
what sadness exists for you of a body you can only
see

body acceptance is strange concept
for those of us who love to work
has anything in this world ever been exempt from
change?

Do you fear we get to "acceptance" and then stay the
same?
or perhaps your error is in the definition of
acceptance and settling
and yes, I am settling

                into

                        love

you see the difference between acceptance and
settling
one is love and one is not love

and if you don't love, then let me be clear
the answers you are looking for aren't on my body

I wonder if I give myself enough credit?
        I wonder if I give myself any credit?
it takes a long time to do the work
the work is hard.
it takes time because it takes time to do
not because there is anything wrong with you
    you are injured and you are healing
you are not lazy, you are a human being
      life is a practice
both a noun and a verb
a practice like in yoga
gentleness and kindness
listening to your body
a verb
the coming back to it
living one more day
finding a way back to yourself
discovering once more
the joy of being alive

An empty page

can be

like the feeling of debilitating anxiety

what do I write? I can't

I'm stuck. help me.

    but then

in a giant leap of

c o u r a g e

the pen

takes one stroke

and then another

the warmth sinks in

a soothing blanket

snuggled up with words

pause here

a sip of coffee

now,

if we aren't careful

near the end of the page

we can feel stuck again

like

the page is ending and

there is no where for the words

to go

      turn the page

and

a a a h h h h , a release

let all the expectations go

and

breathe

It's 5 am and the house is quiet
white lights twinkle in both sides
of my living room
Christmas tree, I'm not done with you
we keep the tree up for our own reasons
I want to be around as many trees as possible
all the time they sustain me
reminding me that I am rooted
inside myself
while the seasons of life
change on the outside
in the other corner of the living room
is a piece of driftwood with a v on top
there, I have wrapped white fairy lights
did you know that you are made of light?
it's 6 am and I light a candle
the scent of fresh linen
pulls me into my mother's arms.
It's suddenly Sunday and I am ten years old and we
are taking the laundry down from where it's been
bathing in the sunlight
as an adult, I don't ever hang up
my laundry anymore
I have my own way of
bringing the light inside.

Yesterday, I found myself
with a case of the hiccups
for no reason
do you remember how
uncomfortable hiccups are?

the whole body is controlled
by the breath

the lungs rattle
sporadically
a ball appears in the chest
it's forced all the way up
a game of volleyball
being played
hic'

as a baby, you endured hiccups
with no understanding of
what was going on
if you can mange hiccups
you can manage anything
you are strong
'cup
you are enough

I used to think that if I
stopped thinking anxious thoughts
it was like living in la la land
with blinders on

> Do you not see the world?
> Everything is on fire!
> I cannot look at this lake
> This one lake
> I cannot focus on its qualities
> That's cheating
> It's not accurate
> Do not placate me
> I am not a child!

Now

    I stop

        and look around

The lake is not on fire
People are living near the lake
I turn and focus on the mountains
They are not on fire either

Anxiety gives me a lighter and says:
        Go!
Look - at - all - the - things
        We - can - burn

And I have looked around
I have seen red
I have burned the world
As we rode our motorbikes down the
Highway to hell

Mindfulness whispers, "stop."

stop the bike
look around
the lake is blue and the sky is blue
birds are singing and people are too

I am safe.
The world is not a bad place.

Mindfulness reminds us to set the gasoline down and use a lighter to light a candle

Watch it burn

Return to this moment.

Return.

Sometimes we can pick
and scrape and peel
parts of a conversation
until the pieces fit our
judgements, stories of
how surely that person
must have felt at that time

the words said at a meeting
though cut deep
do not burn into our skin forever

instead
keep
your
peace

and think, "this does not belong to me"
keep energy in rooms and
disregard the compulsion
to gossip about sideways glances
these things fill your teeth
lungs and belly with
preoccupations and stress
let them go
yes, they may have belonged
to you a moment ago
but they don't belong to you
anymore

I laugh loudly and never cover my mouth
or hide my smile
I sing when I am happy
just made up songs narrating
what I am doing
I stop
      when people talk
pause
my work to give

 undivided
             attention, most of the time
I don't wear make-up at work
someone commented to me
"I admire how you don't care about what others think
about you"
oh,
it's not that I don't care,
I just don't consider
someone else's opinion as more significant than my
own
my worth is defined by me alone
production doesn't increase if I wear make up
or a sports jacket or thirty pieces of flare
anyway
I am concerned about connection, not production
I am a human, not a worker bee
freedom to be me, now that is luxury

Where the ocean meets the sand
my nose nestles in, grabbing all my
beachside memories and
my brain lights up with joy.

The scent of saltwater sinks
to the top of my nose
I breathe in deep to pull it close
deeper and deeper and deeper again

I close my eyes and I am there.
Sand is warm beneath my feet
my body is wrapped in a light salty spray
ah! peace and so many beautiful feelings

Memories are wonderful that way
you don't have to be stuck in the bad ones
invite the good ones back to play
take a deep breath and be on your way.

Are you ready to love,
not as a mom but as a woman?
a woman is not concerned
about where he goes
or who he texts
          a mom is
a woman doesn't set a curfew
          a mom does
a woman doesn't accept
late nights, no calls, drunk texts
d i s r e s p e c t
          a mom has no choice
          but to love and love again
              no matter what the sin
Are you a mom or a woman to this lover?
a woman says

                    yes
                   there
                   more
                    of
                   that
                    I
                   want
                    it
                    all
                   don't
                   stop

a mom is giving
she puts others first

a woman does not keep score
she knows her worth and she
decides for herself and she says no.

do not love your partner like your children
it's a different love

I know that it's the only love
you've ever been shown and
it's the only love you've ever known
but
there is more to love
than what you know to claim for yourself
at this point in time

there is more to love
than giving every single piece of you
until it's gone

that's not love,
     that's a country song

His honesty is healing
every time he says an
uncomfortable truth,
I recognize courage and respect
the hairs on my skin perk up
and they whisper, "we are safe"

his hands are helping
we don't keep score
of whose mess belongs to who
we just do

his smile makes my heart smile
and purr

the only thing is
he stays up late and starts snoring
at 5am when he comes to bed
it wakes me up
through my earplugs

I always wanted a nudge
to write in the morning

Sundays at 8:00pm

                          I stop

           Pour a warm bath

Put down the washcloth

And the pen

And the just one more thing

                          I stop

My cue is to throw the ball

Into the tub and breathe in

I have done enough

Before, that, 7:40pm

My alarm goes off cuing me to

Start

    S l o w i n g   d o w n

In the tub, I touch my feet together

My roots greet each other

I ground and leave my

           Distracted mind

For all these mindful moments

My toes are sea anemones

My knees make waves

 I have a thought: I want to check

My phone to see if I spelled

Sea anemones right

I try to resist the lure of my phone
                    Resistance is futile
          It's a practice

I notice: I am having a thought,
"I want my cell phone"

I can breathe
                    Breathing helps me notice my
body
Don't fight - refocus

Sea anemones

The wind howls outside my window
I am safe

       Behind two paned glass and
       Insulation, a sturdy Canadian duplex, 1964
Three blankets
And cotton sheets
With a hedgehog liking her lips
Sitting on my chest

       My breathing slows and I become aware
       Of her experience. I want her to feel safe
too.

One two three four
              Pause
One two three four
              Pause

An itch appears on my brow
If I react to scratch it, it frightens the hedgehog

I have to feel into it, this discomfort
       What does it feel like, exactly?
       What components is it made of?
       Where, exactly, is it on my brow?
       How slowly can I start to move my arm?

Breathing gently

One two three four

      Pause

One two three four

      Pause

The arm moves slowly

I check the feeling again.

It's stopped.

I am not my thoughts.

Charlotte in her garden 2019

Of all the planets in the solar system
you came to be on this one
you don't have to do anything
you already are
a walking, talking miracle
there is no waste
of space
of life
those thoughts are lies, actually

there is nothing for you to do
only smile if you want to
do not adorn yourself
for the entertainment of others
unless you enjoy it

remind yourself everyday:
life is a gift,

you don't have to earn it.

you deserve to be here
which means more than you deserve to take up space
here or breathe here

more than just to breathe here
but dream here

yes, my dear, I'm saying you deserve to have the life
you've always wanted

you're allowed to adorn your body in a way that
you've always fancied

darling, you have nothing to fear
you deserve to be here
you deserve to be seen here
you deserve to have your life here

you do not have to believe me
for something to be true

for millennia we thought we were the only planet in
the universe
and when we changed to learn something new
the world revolted

it stands to be true
there will a revolution in you
and you will see the truth

there is a reason for you

you have a destiny
                        it's time to believe.

I write poetry in the morning
words are the instrument
that I practice playing with
they are the lighthouse
that lights the way
in the deep recesses of fog
that is my mind

in the morning, I sit in stillness
the bitter taste of coffee
a green velvet dress in my mouth
squinting my eyes
tremors of chill cascade down my back
it's winter and my body wants rest

we had moved from the city lights
from being woken up at 6:30am
garbage trucks outside the window
people milling about
alarm clocks from our neighbours
traffic in the morning
to the suburbs

buy a house in front of a school
better resale value, they said
things seem so simple on paper
everyday at 6:30am the snowblowers

come to blow the snow from

in front of the school
                by 7:15am, I am still
                already exhausted
                by machines

7:20am and my alarm tells me that it's time
to move away from these pages and into
the next phase of machines
I don't feel connected today

time is a currency in this man-made place
days like today are difficult to accept
how far we've split away
from connection to ourselves
and the rest of the human race

Please note that you can
turn off
the news
the notifications
the phone
and still be a productive
member of society
please note that you are
a human and not a machine
don't let the media break you
you are always in control of what
messages you receive
we live in a warzone, information overload
everything is tragic and all the time and getting
worse
it doesn't make you ignorant
to turn it off
it makes you smart
and self-aware and respectful
of what you need
do not put money into
every vending machine you see
nor your time into following politicians like
celebrities

This is a slow day of

languid longing for peace

oh, can you see?
        b r e a t h e
and peace is here
        bring it inside
nestle between these words
you have worked enough
you have done your best
here is your permission
      r e s t

I call my boundaries from the earth
deeper still
from caverns and cenotes
can you hear me?
I call my boundaries from her ancestors
red cedar tree
800 years old
from Stanley Park, Vancouver
I call the tree that sits outside my door
waiting for me
I press my feet firmly
to the ground and I feel her energy
her runners coming to meet
my bones
and strengthen
my core
building up and leaving
buds in their place
new ideas
potential
I call my boundaries from the Earth and I hear them –
clear as day
solid as
m o u n t a i n s

The four sides of my mouth
                    and the four places they attach
        is it two sides?
and now a debate in my monkey mind
    there is chaos, chaos, chaos

sliding around all the uses of my time
                    I can't really decide and don't
so, I go from screen to screen and slide from seat to
seat – I feel electric and electrifying

 like a child
wait see what I can do
wait see my room, my favourite colour
and the classic stall
        … what's *your* favourite colour?
(stalls, I know them all and I still fall)

my monkey mind climbs each tree
each thought
important and more precious than the rest
my precious thoughts and emotions

oh monkey, when will you rest?

Guess what?
   with a grin

     just tell me bro
some of us don't like surprises
and others don't feel safe enough to joke

There is someone in my life
we have weird energy
nothing's wrong
    exactly
       but it just makes me feel ...
maybe if I could decide on that
I could decide what to do

We can certainly cope with life alone
but why, when others have been there too
some family you choose
others are chosen for you

oh, well I know why
and so do you that sometimes family
aren't so kind especially when they are
always telling you what to do

and friends well they lie don't they
so then, again, we feel alone
lonely and contemplate why we survive
are we wasting this one true gift of life?

we can certainly listen to why
and see the trail of complacency
but this life is not about revelling in sadness
alas, put joyfulness in awe in your pocket

bring them along for the ride
the ride of a lifetime, the time of your life
The life you occupy matters to this world
To beings that you can't perceive or see

your life, where it is, not just where it will be – it
matters to so many people
including me. Your life can be filled with joy and
love and reverie. I believe.

We are sitting on the edge of a century
Teetering between the unfair systems
Which bring us an odd sense of safety
because we know them

And the hope of fairness for the future

Feet on the floor and a big breath in
Hold it hold it hold it hold on so tight

and then
Let it go let it go   let it go

and again, breathe in all our hopes and all your
dreams

Your fears?

Let them go

        let them go

     l

        e

           t

t

h

e

m

g

o

Why do we huddle up and trip
Over each other to buy
Sparkly things and paper
Reminders of love, actually
It's the season for love (remember)

We hold onto other people's pain
thinking we can't get go or they
will feel the whole load and we
need to be responsible because
our superpower is to feel so
why wouldn't it be so?

We hold so tightly to our expectations
how can we start letting it go?
and not fall down the slippery slope
a slovenly meaningless life out of control

to let it go, I imagine that conversation
as the air and into a balloon I blow
I blow and blow all my feelings and thoughts
until I've had enough and then I tie it up

we can carry the balloon as long as we'd like
to school, to work, on a flight
I carry the balloon with me but I don't
take the air back in, which means I'm
less likely to have an emotional reaction

I revisit my balloon to observe its qualities
to take positive purposeful communication
you can even decorate your balloon
red for anger and for sadness, a deeper blue

How long have you been carrying your balloons?

What are they made of: air or cement?
do you spend your time pushing a red wagon
along with your balloons that are too heavy to take?
conversations weighing on your body
for so long it might break?
or do you choose a few balloons to settle on
and let the others fall away?

It's your choice today
Gather your thoughts, put them in a balloon
and let them float away
Give yourself permission to let it go, it's ok
breathe in clean air

and breathe it all away

breathe in clean air

and breathe it all away

breathe in clean air

and breathe it all away

It's quiet this morning
Soft vanilla and crisp peppermint waft
Through my senses and mmmm coffee
I am a joyful container of love

I sit, feet firmly rooted to the ground
The Earth feels my connection
Through my body and ahhhh grounded
I am one with Mother Earth

I breathe and take oxygen into my lungs
The life force of the planet cycled
Through time and space and atmosphere
I am the planet, and the planet is me

I breathe in and out slowly thanking
Each tree, by type, if not by name
Thank you to each tree and plant for making the air
that I need

And as I do that, I visualize a lofty tree
Inside of me, tall and strong and proud
Tipping its leaves to the sun to soak in
Sunshine and happiness and life force

When I am ready, when I am full
I thank the tree and let it go
I put my feet firmly on the ground
And when I stand, I stand tall

And what of me?
this year has gone so fast
all those early mornings and late-nights
sometimes spent drawing circles
other times, mindful (still, I can't remember)
and what of you this last year?
gentle with yourself as you reflect on your progress
success is only one word
here are a few more: lived, breathed, experienced
survived, recovered,
recorded, held, felt, enjoyed

each year, instead of a goal or a thing to do
something more to be, achieve or see
I select a word [compassion]
mindfully place it in my heart
and use it to update all my passwords
and what of time?
only a man-made construct
assembled for trade and commerce
there are lots of languages outside of time
like poetry and dance
and horses

When I think of time, I feel so small
The work never seems to end!
So much is left to do!
I like this to remember this:
I am living on a small rock, covered with water and
billions of lifeforms
In the middle of space where time is just a theory
(you are too)

And what would we do if we suddenly woke up and
our
problems have gone away: one giant family, together

Would we still be fighting over where we go after we
die?
Because, at the core of all of this, you know that's the
argument, right?

(By doing this, we miss this life.)

Imagine us, 100 years ago
All of this hadn't been invented yet
Some see that we have come so far
And others, say, actually, not at all

I see hope here
We are waking up to
Different possibilities and accountability
And the world of who we are: humans
Loving not only our children but also ourselves
It feels like a blank page: 2020
Where nothing is written yet and the world waits
Holds its breath
As ink slowly seeps in, marking moments
You understand that we are the world, right?

You know the time isn't actually 2020, right?
The Earth is actually 5.5 billion years old
Time is just a creation someone made 2020 years ago
When you feel like you are running out of time,
remember
It isn't actually real

I ran a half-marathon in Vancouver a few years ago
We went through Stanley Park
It was so breathtakingly beautiful that people stopped
their race
To watch the mountains and to take pictures.
You can stop, anytime, in the race of your life.
You can stop and you do not even need to tell anyone
why.

When I was little time had no meaning
the last 20 years have gone past in a second
So, maybe that means that time doesn't have
meaning
Which means: you still have time

You are more than your goals
You do not have to produce anything
Here, let's enjoy this life together

We want to run so fast inside ourselves
when we have finished running away
we pull ourselves apart and then stitch ourselves
together so hard and aggressively
like our planet like our cities
we go to war with everything
trying to beat our agenda into submission
but you cannot hate yourself into loving yourself
the messiness, imperfections, missed chances,
unlucky roles, mistakes, bad decisions
you are not the sum of who you are
just like all the shipwrecks in the ocean
don't become the Ocean
no, they fall away.

 The Ocean stays
magnificent and full of magic
just like you.

For five minutes this morning, I just sat
On the stairs
Waiting for the time to go by
Thinking of how to change: myself, my house
And a strong voice said: stop
How are you, really?
We distract with all this
   Stuff
       I need to stop travelling through my mind
staring at the way

I have too many plans to waste time here on exactly
the eighth chair
The light casts itself against the wall
And I sit
Transfixed

Well, at least one of us is happy

I was always afraid of blank pages
What if I made a mistake?
But now that I am older, I fear:
What if I make nothing?

I have always wanted a sister
Someone who could help me
Put up all my certificates in my office
And make my life a touch more glamourous
I now realize that I have sisters
And have had them this entire time

For a long time I was embarrassed and so I walked
alone and in longing
Do you ever feel your life
Literally turning a new chapter?

A cosmic lift!

!

f

f

O

that stuck page to a fresh life

Ah!

The page releases all that weight
of the past and a new story begins

It is so deliciously intoxicating that you dive into your
new life right away
and you don't even remember that old life anymore
and it does not bother you at all.

Winter is when the sky is white
And the floor is white
And everything is grey
Except for the sparkles on houses
That light up the way

There is no place to be but here
wherever here is for you
in your pyjamas watching Bob's Burgers all-day
or climbing a mountain
don't look around for a different life to live
you get your life and that's magical
one person would absolutely love to have
just one lazy day.
you are allowed to enjoy your life.

The mountains touch our hearts
with the pulse of their breath
she's created herself to be timeless,
nurtured by the sun
Mother Earth watches her creations blossom
with her unwavering all-seeing eye from above
A hawk, an eagle, a majestic bird of prey
nothing goes unnoticed in her world
including our attempts at intruding on her
imperfections
and in our trying to make
things pure and symmetrical, we fail
she lets her tears fall slowly bathing us in a soft rain.
We think we have all the answers to her plight
Mother Earth, is it too late to help you?
I'd like to think no. That it is early days still where we
can pick up the pieces that we have left on your soil
and stand on the top of a mountain in awe of your
creations including myself, an imperfect human
beautiful soul
made with love by the ultimate creator, thank you
Earth Mother, Mother Earth

You have permission to be lazy
there is nothing wrong with laziness
you are not a means of production
it's actually ok
I know what you're going to say

we have a mission on this earth
and we have so little time
no time to waste
so pick up the pace

I counter that as human beings
rest is crucial in sustainability
we have a responsibility
to take care of our body

of course, there is place
but let's just not do efficiency
just for efficiencies' sake
it is ok to set a lower pace

"What do you do for work?"
I have always hated that question
because I am not a robot with work to do
I am a human.
I am already doing it.
You are too.

Yes, politics are scary
    but cinnamon buns exist
        and first sips of coffee
sunsets, waterfalls, beaches, and neighbours
oh, and hugs and kisses and wagging tails

You do not remember who you are
and that's not your fault
This place, this planet of ice and stone and loneliness
Promised you that if you forgot, you would be alright
The biggest lie it's the biggest lie they told you
Give up your power, they said, and be who we say
And you held on so tightly for so many years
But one day, they took it from you.
Us women, we've been raped, and murdered,
and beaten. We've been tortured, and burned, and
cracked into submission
Our wombs, our sacred places have been ripped apart
By them, those who saw our power and were terrified
and then we started to hide in caves, inside ourselves,
we started to tuck passions into pockets,
we took new names
we assessed our talents and gifts as part of this world
they are not of this world, my dear sister, your gifts
you are not of this world, my dear sister, your soul
bright and light and deadly is your real power
that was stolen from you as a little girl.
Woman! Hear my call, you belong with us together
Woman! Hear my call, we are meant to be together
You can stand in your power once again
It is your birthright.
Dear sister, we are here, answer our call

You will find us naked in the woods, dancing
unapologetically
One with the earth and wrapped in Mother Nature's
embrace
Dear sister, I remember you and you belong with us

Today is the first of three days
that seem like an eternity
three years rather than three days
that I might get the news
of your arrival

these days have come like this
for seasons, then years
and years from a lifetime before

I don't know anymore
I do know somethings though
like the first buds always come
during spring and that are things
that I can do
                    So, I do
I take a big breath in
And I write to you
I imagine the things that we would do
colouring or singing songs
or making paper cranes
it has all been imagined inside my head
since I was fourteen years old
and I learned what my body could do
how easy it seemed at that time
they said it could only take one time
when it's been years
and I've been missing you
          What can I do?

I started off in this world a careful being
choosing only things that were happy and clean
a good girl, a good daughter, a good eater
children should be heard and not seen

I started out with plans that were made
someone else mapped out the way for me
to be good, to listen well, and to follow a path
that would ensure safe travels on my journey

If I painted my life and got it down
with my life-intention planned: to be good
there are so many times I coloured outside the lines
and felt guilty for not doing things that I should

the cracks and glass I stumbled through
served to break me at the time
I learned how to put them back together
and how to have peace with what's mine

It took some time to figure out that good
wasn't the only goal to be
that there could be good in messy places
and that there was room in life to be me

I discovered the thrill of colouring outside the lines
of creating things just for their own discovery

191

the deep scars of my life became the map
to help me find my way back to me

if someone were to look at my whole life
as a movie or a giant story, what would they see?
a quest for good and perfect and nice
and ending with the happiness and joy of being me

Release the expectations for yourself
that you always have to be perfect, kind, and pretty
your story has cracks and imperfections
and you are the one who decides who you want to be

We cannot go back, only forwards
so, forwards
              we
                   will go
          with
                loving
                       kindness
may your compassion
include yourself
may your loving
include yourself

May you include yourself in your own life.

There is light inside of you
think of rock like a geode
quartz crystals, banded agate
her inside world is dark
until a force shocks the rock
and comes out with beautiful colours
and her light shines so brightly
have you ever felt that happen to you?
what kind of rock inspires you?
There is still light, no matter how
many scars sit on top of your heart
look no further than a tree
his hardened trunk is a hidden storyland
scars, blemishes, and constant seasons
on his top, yet firm he stands
rooted and tall. have you ever felt that
you were made to withstand?
Inside of you is a whole family of trees
resolute and strong, a family of mother Earth
a family in which you belong
If you were a tree, which tree would you be?
Imagine it for a moment for me.

No matter what you failed to do or
what happened to you, your ancestors
would be proud of you. For you are
eighty grandmothers into your family line.

You have made it this far and still you survive!
(or perhaps you thrive and are thrilled to be alive)

When was the last time you felt happy
and joyful and free? Take a few breaths to
remember it now here with me.
It's ok if that memory was long go
all that matters is that you know
you can access happiness anytime.

Your memories and feelings are like clouds
they come and they go
underneath is your heart and soul
the light you have can always show
smile with your eyes and you will know
these gentle truths that I know.

The old ways are fading
I feel it with all my being
We are peeling and bringing
Light into ourselves
The old systems are cracking
Our hearts are singing
Rise up and be seen
It's time.
It's our time.

I owe my cousin a letter
its weight feels like too many sweaters
I do not like owning anything yet if you looked at my
lifestyle, you'd think I'd very much like owing things
because I have so much to owe: to banks, to people,
to work, to my friends, to my family, and to myself.
If we choose our life and how it goes then
how did I end up with so many owes?
my life is filtered through a life of lack
always trying to do more, be more, achieve more
to make up for what I lack
this is a poor plan of attack
and just like that I understand my quandary
the next big hurdle, mountain, upgrade, space
is not going to move if I reform myself
actually, the old self has to die to expose
the sapphire inside
Once the filter is removed then life can thrive
it is not a skill, an ability to release, a practice
though they all facilitate and lay witness
the old self has to die
for the new self to be able to thrive
we are scared of change it is because we know the
feeling of loss and letting go
we have built our lives
there is so much at stake
there is no time to make a mistake

time marches on and the time for
self-love and self-care grows shorter
and now we have to plan a funeral?
And clean the closet? And do the paper work?
It is all too much.
I understand.
I continue to rock on the choppy seas of life
back and forth in a forward direction
until one day
I make a decision
to get off the boat

   And I get into the water and I float.

Being a human is more than what you can do
It is a graceful dance between present you
And someone you will never meet: future you
Have you ever received a gift from the past?
A piece of clothing you saved or some cash
Did you thank her, that she of the past?
She who sacrificed in that moment for you
When the work gets hard to do
The make up stops getting removed
The self-care routine is out of tune
Remember her, the future version of you
Even when you can do nothing, there is something
you can do
Wash your feet before you go to bed
Comb your hair and rest your head
thank her, past you, for all that you did
and promise future you that you will begin again
brightening her skin
            embracing a new day
                    washing the past away
until the day
when future you is thanking you.

Stef Guilly is an optimist, artist, and joyful poet from Edmonton, AB Canada. She is the mother of Somatic Poetry: an interactive feeling experience. You can find out more about her work at www.StefGuilly.com.

Patreon.com/StefGuilly Instagram @StefGuilly

Made in the USA
Middletown, DE
15 October 2021

50118200R00116